A

HEALING

GRIEF

A HEALING GRIEF

Walking
with Your Friend
Through Loss

Sara Wengerd

Foreword by Larry Kehler

**Herald
Press**

Scottdale, Pennsylvania
Waterloo, Ontario

Library of Congress Cataloging-in-Publication Data
Wengerd, Sara, 1942-
A healing grief : walking with your friend through loss / Sara Wengerd.
        p. cm.
Includes bibliographical references.
ISBN 0-8361-9198-6 (pbk. : alk. paper)
1. Grief—Religious aspects—Christianity. 2. Bereavement—
Religious aspects—Christianity. 3. Wengerd, Sara, 1942- I. Title.

BV4330 .W46 2002
155.9'37--dc21
        2001007267

The paper used in this publication is recycled and meets the minimum
requirements of American National Standard for Information Sciences—
Permanence of Paper for Printed Library Materials, ANSI Z39.48-1984.

Scripture is from the New Revised Standard Version Bible, copyright 1989,
by the Division of Christian Education of the National Council of the
Churches of Christ in the USA, and is used by permission.

Dedication

To Heidi and Kristin,
who shared the losses

Contents

Foreword

In the year 2000 I helped to gather and edit a resource collection for pastors and other church-related caregivers on death, dying, and dealing with grief. It was a Mennonite Church Canada endeavor. They named it, *Going Gracefully*. In working at this project I realized how important it is for us as individuals, families, and churches to be in much closer touch with the realities of death and grief.

Sara Wengerd has given us a remarkable gift in writing about the various stages of her and her family's grief experiences following her husband John's sudden death. *A Healing Grief* is a wake-up call for all of us to stop being in denial about death and grief. We need to face it and help one another to deal with it.

Sara's forthright look at her experiences during the first few days after John's death, as well as during the first year and beyond, provides us with many helpful insights and suggestions. The "How to Be Helpful" sections which follow each chapter offer excellent advice on how neighbors, family members and congregations can be helpful to grieving persons.

We need to remember that grief does not end at the conclusion of the first annual cycle of remembering. Recognizing this, we need to find ways of acknowledging the grief in special ceremonies and by being in touch with the grieving on special anniversaries and other occasions.

A Healing Grief is an important and timely resource for us all.

—*Larry Kehler*
Winnipeg, Manitoba

Preface

Many of us are hesitant or awkward in approaching a recently bereaved person. We are afraid of saying the wrong words or causing the person to become emotional. Since grief is experienced in such individual ways, we are unsure what is needed or wanted by this particular person.

Because I remember my own uncertainty in reaching out to persons who had suffered loss before I experienced the death of my husband, I think it will be helpful to share what my family found comforting during those first days, the funeral, and all the changes that were to come. Many of the acts of kindness that were supportive to us were new ideas to me, small gestures that were immeasurably useful in helping us to cope with our losses. Most people appreciate a listening ear, talking about their loved one, eating with others, or practical assistance. Often, I have found it most useful to ask directly what a grieving person would like from me.

Writing this book helped me to understand how the profound experience of the death of a spouse has changed my life and the lives of my daughters. I gained a new appreciation for the relationship that John and I shared and for the kindness of my friends and family. I felt grateful for God's comfort in ways that I could understand.

It is my hope that *A Healing Grief* can offer ideas to friends and family about ways to be supportive to a hurting person. Perhaps the bereaved will find it useful in communicating what they need to survive and in coming to the understanding that their feelings and fears are valid. Professionals may get a deeper sense of the "feel" of loss. Wearing two hats—that of a hospice nurse and that of a grieving person—combines these different perspectives.

I wish to thank my friends Helen Alderfer, Rachel Hartzler, and Glenn Barclay for reading the manuscript and suggesting helpful changes. My daughters, Heidi and Kristin, were encouraging, and our discussions about the book helped me to understand how difficult they found the death of their father. Thanks to my editor, Sarah Kehrberg, for her affirmation and practical guidance.

One becomes vulnerable when writing autobiographically. It is my prayer that my exposure can comfort a survivor or suggest a helpful course of action to a friend or relative accompanying a bereaved person on the holy road of grief.

In the same way, the Spirit
helps us in our weakness.
We do not know what we ought to
pray for, but the Spirit himself
intercedes for us with groans that
words cannot express.

—Romans 8:26

The First Day

There are days in our lives that change us forever, watershed days, days which clearly mark before . . . and after. Today has dawned bright and beautiful in the mountains of western Maryland and Pennsylvania, as I drive home from my night job as a hospice nurse. I feel like a zombie, struggling to stay awake and not run off the road, as I have several times in the past. I am alert enough to notice how spring wanes, the higher I drive into the mountains. Though desperately sleepy, I stop to check on the elderly residents of a low-income housing facility that I manage as my second part-time job. There are no problems requiring immediate attention, so I gratefully drive home to bed, unmindful of the trauma that is to come.

My head barely touches the pillow when the doorbell rings. In my drowsy state, I try to ignore its clamor, but the voice of Budd, my brother-in-law, arouses me. His voice is urgent,

"Sara, John fell, and he's unconscious." To the wife of a roofing contractor, such news is alarming. I drop to the step, unable to stand. My heart is racing, and I feel like an observer of someone else's bad news. "We must go to him," I say, "but I can't drive, since I worked all night."

I lift up my eyes to the hills—
from where will
my help come?
My help comes from the Lord,
who made heaven
and earth.
—Psalm 121:1-2

While Budd drives home to change clothes, causing what feels like an unnecessary delay, I arrange with John's foreman to drive us to the hospital. The sober expressions on the faces of John's employees just returning from the work site, tell me more than I want to know. In response to my questions, they reluctantly relate the story of John's forty-foot fall from the peak of a barn roof. The arrival of the ambulance took only minutes, then the rescue squad tried earnestly to resuscitate him. Realizing that his spinal, head, and internal injuries were massive, they phoned for the life flight helicopter to rush him to a trauma center in Johnstown, Pennsylvania, sixty miles away.

Minutes seem endless until Budd returns; we then stop at the high school to pick up my youngest daughter, Kristin. This is a time we need to be together, to comfort each other. Just seven weeks ago today, her special friend, Jeff, died in his sleep of an undiagnosed heart infection. She is still grieving, and I dread to tell her that she may lose her father and special comforter too.

Kristin and I clasp hands in the backseat during the hour drive through the Allegheny Mountains of western Pennsylvania. My greatest fear is not that John will be dead, but that we have lost the husband and father we knew as he clings to life by artificial means. I pray for him and for the wisdom and strength to face what lies ahead.

Upon our arrival at the hospital, we are ushered into a small room in the emergency department. Our pastor, John's close friend, has come to be with us. With grave faces the bearded ER physician and a social worker enter the room. "We did all we could, but we couldn't save your husband," the physician says with a kind voice. I feel numb. Tears gather in Budd's eyes, and the pastor starts to weep. My first coherent thought is, "Now Jeff is not alone." Two tragedies so close together seem overwhelming and unfair. "May we see him?" I finally ask. "Yes," says the physician, taking my arm. Kristin and the pastor join us.

I do not know what to expect. The only visible mark is a gauze bandage covering a scalp laceration. But John's face is inflated like a balloon, making him hard to recognize. I am to learn later from my sister, an ER nurse, that head trauma causes edema (swelling) of the face. "Oh, God," I whisper in disbelief. I touch his arm, and the sheet covering him moves aside, revealing a needle still inserted in his arm. I shudder to think of all the heroic measures that were used to breathe life into him, measures neither of us would have sanctioned had we been given the choice.

We leave the hospital dazed and shaken. "I can't believe what's happened," I repeat over and over, unable to grasp the events of the past two hours. This feels like a nightmare from which we will surely awaken. How will I tell Heidi, my eldest daughter, who is taking final exams as a second-year college student? I feel so weary from my lack of sleep, yet am on full alert from the adrenaline surging through my veins.

A phone call from the hospital by John's foreman alerted the community, and our neighbors and two close friends are waiting for us at our home. My first tears come as my friends embrace me, shedding tears of their own. Our family doctor who is also a close friend has closed his office and is here. He phoned the hospital and knew long before we did that John is dead. John's family and our close friends come to sit with us. Food arrives.

We must inform Heidi, away at college, before she learns about her father's death from someone else. I call the director of students and ask her to find Heidi and tell her of the fatal accident. Heidi confesses later that she was sure she had committed some misdemeanor when the director of students, the vice president, and the college president came to her door. In a few minutes she returns my call, and I tell her we are trying to make arrangements for her to come home. Jeff's mother and sister volunteer to make the three-hour trip to Virginia and leave immediately. This is an especially generous offer, because memories of trips to visit Jeff at the same school will be fresh and painful.

I want to inform my family personally of John's death. My widowed mother lives alone, so I phone close friends of the family who are able to be with her as they tell her she has lost a son-in-law. I call my sister in Albuquerque, a brother-in-law in Ann Arbor, and a brother in Nairobi, Kenya, assuring him that I do not expect him to return for the funeral.

Budd phones John's brother in Pittsburgh and his sister in Phoenix. He also calls extended family members. I phone two college friends I've kept in close touch with for thirty years.

Word spreads quickly throughout the community and across the country. A pastor friend from eastern Pennsylvania prays with me over the phone. More friends gather at the house, their anguished tears and stricken faces a confirmation of what I am feeling but am too numb to express. Later I will not remember everyone who came in those hours of shock, but I will remember the comfort and feeling of solidarity their presence brought.

There is suffering and darkness in our lives, but that suffering cannot put out the reality of God. Instead, the presence of God lights the way through our suffering.
—Doris Longacre

My dear friend, Es, has been here for hours, quietly accepting food and recording the donors. She warms some soup and gently serves me on a tray. I can only manage to swallow a few spoonfuls of soup, but her loving care is like salve to a wound. In the hazy days to follow, her presence is one of the few things I remember. She organizes our meals, using donated food, and keeps the household functioning while I attend to funeral planning and greeting guests.

Heidi arrives. Her friends will pack her belongings and bring them when they come for John's funeral; she has had no closure to her school year and will be transferring to a new school in the autumn. She and I greet each other dry-eyed. Has she inherited my emotional reserve? We seem to be unable to cry in public, which will later prompt one of the residents of the elderly housing complex I manage to remark, "You were just like Jackie Kennedy."

When my spirit grows faint within me, it is you who know my way.
—Psalm 142:3

Bedtime becomes a poignant moment, because for the first time, John's absence cannot be denied. My daughters appear at the bedroom door, saying they want to sleep in my room. One climbs in bed with me while the other spreads a sleeping bag on the floor. It is as though we are circling the wagons to keep out the enemy—death. Sleeping closely together comforts us all.

How to Be Helpful During the First Day

1. If you are a relative, neighbor, or close friend, do go to the house immediately upon learning of the death. Little talking is necessary. An embrace and tears are more welcome than words. Your mere presence shares your friend's grief.

2. Relatives and friends may need to be met at the airport or train station.

3. Bring food. Your friend is paralyzed and without energy to organize meals. Just one dish in a disposable container for immediate or later use could be helpful. Coffee, tea, paper products, soups, breakfast casseroles, breads, cold meats, cheeses, cookies, and fresh fruit are good choices.

4. A house "manager" is very useful. This person can answer the door and phone, keep a record of food donors for thank-you notes later, and heat and serve food for family and guests. A quiet organizing presence relieves the bereaved of the stress of entertaining.

5. If you live at a distance, call and pray over the phone with the bereaved, if prayer seems appropriate.

6. Offer to accompany the family member to the funeral home if he or she must go alone.

7. Be available to phone relatives and friends who live at a distance.

Fear not, for I have redeemed you;

I have summoned you by name;

You are mine.

When you pass through the waters,

I will be with you;

And when you pass through the rivers,

They will not sweep over you.

When you walk through the fire,

You will not be burned;

The flames will not set you ablaze.

—Isaiah 43:1-2

The Second Day

Shock continues today and will temper the sharp pain of loss for many months to come. Losing a spouse must compare with trying to walk with one leg; a part is missing, and it is difficult to keep one's balance. With John's death, I have lost my best friend. Now I have no lover. I have no one to share daily joys and sorrows without much explanation needed. He has been a gentle, affirming father to Heidi and Kristin. Often his jokes and humor have shattered the tension of conflicts, as we all burst into laughter, or he has mediated a dispute between a daughter and me. As an optimist, his glass has been half full; mine is often half empty.

How will I support myself financially and pay college expenses? John understood money management, paying the bills, and investing our savings. Now budgeting and finance will be my tasks—foreign territory. I know very little about cars.

Who will help to make family decisions, mow the lawn, or plant hundreds of flowers each spring? Still the tears don't come. My sense of loss is too deep for tears, which seem to be a trivial expression of my pain.

John and I were opposites, which according to marriage therapists attracts partners to one another. His easygoing humor gave a balance to my more intense, serious nature. He taught me to laugh, and we shared a keen love of travel that recently took us to Jamaica to celebrate our twenty-fifth wedding anniversary. We had faced some significant struggles, especially about where to live, and had worked hard to maintain communication and caring without losing our individual identities. Our love for each other was deep, and I would soon discover that the intimacy of marriage cannot be duplicated by any other relationship.

I met John as a senior nursing student. He was studying at our church's seminary, not to become a pastor, but to find a relevant faith. In that he succeeded, and throughout the rest of his life, his lay ministry was highly valued. I was dating his roommate, but when this relationship faltered, John took the role of peacemaker. When it became clear that his roommate and I had no future, John began asking me to meet him for coffee or to walk along the river. His gentleness and humor immediately attracted me, but I had no intention of getting involved with another man so soon. After a few months of dating, he announced he would marry me. "Not so fast," I said to myself and took a much more cautious approach.

Most of our courtship was by correspondence while he traveled with a Christian youth team in the western United States. By spring we were engaged, and then we married in August of 1965. It was the happiest day of my life, and the wedding photos capture our joy.

While he finished seminary, I worked as a labor and delivery room nurse, and we lived simply but comfortably on my small salary. After he graduated, we moved to Edmonton, Alberta, Canada, where he worked for the provincial government to market Native Canadians' arts and handicrafts, and I taught obstetrics in a large hospital school of nursing. It was a time of establishing our marriage apart from extended family. I still maintain contact with friends we met there.

I called on your name, O Lord, from the depths of the pit. You came near when I called you, and you said, "Do not fear."
—Lamentations 3:55, 57

At the end of two years in Edmonton, we sailed from Vancouver for eleven months of travel around the world. John and I spent many winter evenings discussing our itinerary and planning the details. We purchased all of our international travel before departure so that we would not be stranded penniless in some remote village. The trip was one of the highlights of our marriage, especially in view of the fact that we will never travel together in retirement. I have been grateful many times for our mutual desire for adventure which enabled us to set aside buying a home and beginning a family for the thrill of seeing the Sydney Opera House or climbing the terraced hills of Nepal in a rickety local bus together.

As we visited his family in Pennsylvania after our return to the United States, two of John's brothers asked him to join the family roofing business. I was much less enthusiastic, and we never came to full agreement on the merits of living in Somerset County, a fact with which I had to wrestle after John's death.

> *Listen to your life. See it for the fathomless mystery that it is. In the boredom and pain of it no less than in the excitement and gladness; touch, taste, smell your way to the holy and hidden heart of it because in the last analysis all moments are key moments, and life itself is grace.*
> —Frederick Buechner

First Heidi, then Kristin were born to us in 1971 and 1973, and I made the decision to be a full-time mother and homemaker. The roofing business grew and thrived, while I tried to make peace with living in a rural area that offered few professional opportunities or cultural attractions. Travel to Pittsburgh or Washington, D.C., then to Costa Rica, Belize, England, and Jamaica broadened our contacts with the outside world. Maintaining friendships with women from other parts of the country and finding a few kindred spirits locally became a life raft for me in a sea of loneliness.

Seventeen years later, I took a refresher course and returned to nursing in 1988. Putting children through college is a costly affair! How glad I am that I upgraded my skills. It could be said now that this was providential. That year we also purchased a life insurance policy for John.

We also prepared a written agreement about the disposition of our home, if we should vacate it. We spent fifteen years renovating and beautifying the stately Pre-Civil War tenant house on the family farm. It is constructed of brick, painted white with gray shutters, and it has double porches across its front façade where the girls sleep in the summer. The grand front entrance with its winding staircase and the wide pine board floors, four fireplaces, and wavy small paned windows reflect another era. We all love this house with its view from the family room of wild deer grazing in the fields. How grateful I am that our affairs are in order!

I awaken slowly and savor a brief moment of normalcy until the reality of what has happened hits me like a kick in the abdomen. Most painful is bedtime which I delay as long as possible, only to lie there with thoughts and fears racing through my head.

This day after John's death my mother and sister arrive from Indiana. Pain is etched on their faces, but they reach out to me with comforting embraces. Mother tells me later that John's death is harder for her than my father's who suffered the indignity of Alzheimer's disease for ten years.

I have requested a plain, oak casket, built by an Amish craftsman; John and I believe that simplicity should guide our preparations for burial. Because of my hospice work, we are both keenly aware that it is not only old people who die, and John has often expressed distaste for elaborate funerals.

Within every loss there are seeds for gain and new beginnings.

—Ira J. Tanner

I am thankful for a sense of peace and clarity of mind as I plan a funeral service to celebrate John's life. Two friends agree to choose recorded music for the prelude. John's brothers accompany me to the funeral home to make arrangements. Friends offer to meet relatives at the airport. It is true; I am not feeling everything at once as my pastor has promised. I suspect the harder road lies ahead.

How to be Helpful on the Second Day

1.   Offer to provide lodging for long-distance friends and relatives often faced with unexpected travel expenses.

2.   Check to see if there are airport or train arrivals that need to be met.

3.   Offer to take care of small children during the funeral or to stay in the family's home to make burglaries less likely.

4. Evaluate the need for groceries or other supplies.

5. Offer to wash the cars of those traveling in the funeral procession.

6. Inquire if funeral clothing needs to be laundered and pressed or shoes shined.

The only security any of us will have,

apart from God, rests in how many people love and

are committed to us—whatever may come.

—Joyce Hollyday

The Visitation

I dread the funeral home visitation (sometimes called a "viewing") that I know can be exhausting, but I feel buoyed by the many expressions of appreciation for John's life and find this ritual comforting. My nursing colleagues, our close friends, John's clients, neighbors, business associates, and many others who have been touched by the goodness of John's life come to share our grief.

Josh, the son of a single mother, whom John befriended, stands beside the casket; he reaches up to touch John's face. Turning away in tears, he runs to the parking lot. A young couple carrying a newborn baby step forward to say that John fell from their barn. The pain that he died at *their* barn is written on their faces. I am touched by their concern and by their own grief. Comments "explaining" John's death seem trite and out of touch with what I am feeling. The bearers of such "wisdom" seem misguided or have had little experience with death. At one point, I tell Budd who has come to check on the girls and me, "If another person tells me *why* John died, I'll punch him in the nose!"

Much more helpful to me are the memories shared or expressions of appreciation for John's life. "He was so kind," or "He was an ornery rascal in high school," feel more personal, more real. Later several people tell me that they came to the funeral home, but the lines were so long that they decided to communicate with our family in some other way. I wonder how many people have crowded into this small funeral home? It must be hundreds passing in front of me with hugs and handshakes.

> *Comforters must be prepared to let the pain of another become their own and so let it transform them.*
> —Gerald Sittser

At my request, a basket of daffodils from our yard, arranged by our neighbor, decorates the casket in lieu of an expensive floral tribute. An embroidered picture of bluebirds with the words, "Enjoy life one day at a time," stands on an easel nearby. The picture, a birthday gift from John's foreman, seems to describe John's life—his enjoyment of bluebirds and his ability to set aside time in his busy schedule to savor life's simple pleasures.

More food arrives at the house, enough to feed both John's family and mine, and our roomy farmhouse becomes a hub of activity. Some of us force ourselves to eat to maintain our strength. More friends and relatives come from out of town. I can't believe Uncle Lowell has left his Iowa farm in planting season to be with us. I'm so grateful. I have no idea where people are sleeping—no idea where the clean sheets have been found. I can't think properly. Some of them must be in motels. I'm so cold; I can't stop trembling. It's as if I've nearly been in an accident or someone has just startled me.

How to Be Helpful During the Visitation

1. Arrange for childcare while the bereaved receive callers at the funeral home.

2. A visit to the funeral home can help both you and the family. Share a memory or tell the family something you appreciated about the person who has died. Refrain from trying to "explain" the death. This can seem irrelevant, even callous, to those who are hurting.

3. Contribute to a memorial fund established by the family.

4. Honor requests for no flowers. Floral arrangements can be sent to the survivors later, on the deceased's birthday or on special anniversaries.

5. Money for a tree or shrub to be planted is a meaningful, living memorial.

The Lord is my rock, my fortress

And my deliverer;

My God is my rock in whom I take refuge.

He is my shield and the horn

Of my salvation, my stronghold.

—Psalm 18:2

The Funeral

Today is cool and blustery—typical capricious spring weather in western Pennsylvania's mountains. Our daffodils are blooming, but it feels cold enough to snow. Close family and friends gather for a private service at the funeral home prior to the burial. Tributes written by John's three brothers and sister, Heidi, Kristin, and myself speak of our love for him. How will we ever live without him? I'd like to kiss him before the coffin lid closes for the last time, but I want a memory of warm lips and his welcoming smile, so I merely touch his sleeve.

My heart cries out as John's employees carry his simple casket to its final resting place. How can we allow the earth to swallow this man? The day and the ground seem so cold and inhospitable. I want to scream, "No. Don't take the last reality of John away from us." But, of course, I am silent.

Stepping into the church, I am surprised and embarrassed to

hear a loud rendition of "The Gift of You" by John Denver. Oh yes, I have handed over the responsibility of the prelude music to John's friend, and they are both Denver fans. A Mozart concerto soon fills the air, a testament to John's varied tastes in music.

Since so many rumors are afloat in the community, I have asked the pastor to explain what is known about John's fall. His golfing partner, our neighbor, reads the obituary with a trembling voice, and another friend recites Longfellow's, "The Day Is Done," from which John often quoted, "I see the lights of the village gleam through the rain and the mist. . . ." During a time of sharing memories, several themes emerge—his faith, his kindness, his peacemaking ability, his love of bluebirds, the easy way he related to children, and how much fun he had in life. The funeral message is in John's own words—excerpts from the sermons he preached at our church over the years. Now we're singing, "Come, Come Ye Saints." I believe that God has received John as one of his saints, but how are we going to survive here without him? At least he will never know the pain of losing a spouse. But what about me, Lord? What about his fatherless daughters?

So many have traveled so far to share this sad time with us. I am grateful for the presence of each person here and want to

> *Blessed are those who mourn,*
> *for they will be comforted.*
> —Matthew 5:4

thank them—one of John's favorite cousins from Georgia, a high school friend from Birmingham, the president and his wife from the college where I serve on the board of trustees, sisters and brothers from around the country, good friends from Ohio, my work colleagues from Baltimore, friends of my family since childhood, and friends of Heidi and Kristin. I visit from table to table, as they eat the lunch, prepared by women of the church. "Your loss is our loss," their words and faces tell me. We are learning that sorrow unites people in ways which joy cannot.

Each death is as unique as each life. Each has its own stamp.

—Nicholas Wolterstorff

How to Be Helpful During the Funeral

1. Offer to care for young children who may disrupt the funeral service.

2. Attend the funeral, because it may help your own grief process, and your presence is supportive to the family.

3. Donate food for a meal at the church.

4. Organize a meal for the guests, if none is provided by a church.

A Day at a Time
One day at a time
is all we need
to take each step
into the uncharted future.
Such space makes room
for all eventualities,
supplies a thread to hold together
the present and the past.
Though shadowed
with uncertainty
we journey on
in the strength of
One who is
unbound by change
yesterday, today,
for ever.
—Robert Dunlop

Changes

During the first weeks after John's death, I feel adrift and fearful. I keep asking myself, "How will I manage everything without John?" I am particularly worried about managing our finances, since John assumed major responsibility for paying the bills and was much more familiar with taxes and investments. Fortunately he recorded all of our assets and shared this information with me. John's brothers have told me that his weekly check will continue to come until the end of the year, and their generosity will help me to pay the bills while we begin to forge our new life. Acknowledging the rawness of my own grief, I have asked for a month's leave of absence from working with hospice patients; I work at my housing management job for a few hours, several times a week, until my concentration wanes or I feel the need to rest.

My mother is staying with us for a week, cooking our meals and keeping the household functioning. She understands the magnitude of losing a spouse, and her presence is helpful and comforting.

Cards and letters flood our mailbox. These messages can be read at our convenience with no expected response, then reread later with a clearer mind. One of the most helpful letters we will receive arrives several months after John's death. It comes at a time when I am asking the *why* questions for which there are no answers. I am also struggling with anger at our situation and, irrational as it may seem, at John for leaving us.

God seems so far away that I have asked my friends to pray in my stead, for I cannot. These sensitive words of our family friend come at just the right time: "I have come to believe that God does not will suffering, that God's Spirit is present and active in the midst of suffering and becomes for us a sustaining power. I believe remembering our blessings and sureties—God's love and grace, the love and support of friends, and our faith and hope—help to carry us. If we listen, I believe suffering can be instructive about life, values, and priorities. Perhaps most of all, I have learned to live with unanswered questions. I have decided it is presumptuous and idolatrous for me to think I can and should be able to always make sense out of life and neatly explain everything."

Carmen, who has come to our farm for twelve summers from a Brooklyn high-rise through the "Fresh-Air Fund," flies from

Boston to mourn with us after her college exams are finished. John is the only father figure she has ever known, so without his teasing and attention she finds the silence and sadness that lingers an adjustment. She photographs every corner of the property as if to capture her memories of happier times.

Three weeks after John's death, my two college friends fly to be with us from Wisconsin and Colorado. The gift of their presence when shock is turning to reality is perfect timing. We listen to a tape of the funeral and cry together. They help me finish scores of "thank-you" notes. Our thirty-year friendship feels like a firm place to stand in a shifting world. Since my concentration and organization are lacking, they help with meal preparation and take us out to eat, just before they leave for the airport.

To live in this world
you must be able
to do three things:
to love what is mortal,
to hold it
against your bones knowing
your own life depends on it;
and when the time comes to
let it go,
to let it go.
—Mary Oliver

Little do we know that a new crisis is looming. Following our final brunch in a restaurant, Mary emerges from the rest room, holding her head and moaning with pain. We help her to the car and race to the local clinic. Lila and I are both alarmed, because we know our stoic friend is in agony. In the examining room, some quick decisions are made. Though I have not driven much since John's death, I am to rush Mary in the back of my car to the emergency room of a large hospital thirty miles away. Lila will return the rental car to the Pittsburgh airport and fly home. She leaves us very reluctantly.

The suffering of the world has worked its way deeper inside me. I never knew that sorrow could be like this.
—Nicholas Wolterstorff

Upon arrival at the emergency department, it is quickly confirmed that Mary has a leaking brain aneurysm and she is placed in ICU, in a dark room on strict bed rest under the care of a neurosurgeon. As a nurse, I am aware that she is at great risk for further hemorrhage. I call her husband, a physician in Colorado, who says he'll arrive as soon as he can book a flight. A friend and our pastor come to sit with me. Unspoken questions about how many more crises we can handle hang in the air. Through gritted teeth, I say to the pastor, "If Mary dies, I will know God is against me." Am I to lose one of my dearest friends as well?

Mary rests quietly and patiently for ten days before surgery can be performed. I make daily visits, and her husband and three children come for the surgery that is successful. She and her daughter return to our home to recuperate before she is able to make the long trip home to Colorado Springs. The only adverse effect of her surgery is the inability to raise one eyebrow due to severed facial nerves. After the losses of the past three months, Mary's recovery feels like a miraculous gift.

Heidi and Kristin live at home this summer. Both have summer jobs, and Heidi takes a biology class in preparation for entering pharmacy school in the autumn. Wanting to continue our traditional summer vacation at the eastern shore, we choose the new location of Cape May, New Jersey. A friend joins us, which rounds out our usual foursome. But the pain of John's absence is even more apparent when we change our daily routines, and I pen in my journal:

> You loved our beach
> Vacations.
> How we are missing
> You
> As we try to enjoy what we did
> Together.
>
> Each ebb and flow
> Of the
> Waves
> Reminds us
> "He is gone."
> "He is gone."

This summer is a blur of meeting with our attorney and accountant, meetings at which I need to take notes to remember that we met at all. Estate settlement is time-consuming and tedious. Each session is a reminder that I am responsible for our affairs, because John has died. Although our assets have increased, I know they must be invested wisely to ensure a college education for the girls and retirement income for me. I mourn the death of dreams for our retirement together and long for respite from so much responsibility.

Our car dies, and I make the first car purchase of my life. Nothing is the same. I rarely cook, and when we do eat together, we sit at the kitchen counter, because we cannot bear to face John's empty chair. We try to protect one another from what we are feeling and have little reserve to share each other's pain. We tend to live parallel lives, following our individual pursuits. At my suggestion we visit a grief counselor together to help us communicate, but Heidi and Kristin prefer not to schedule more appointments.

Come to me, all you who are weary and burdened, and I will give you rest.
—Matthew 11:28

In my journal, I write, "I need to sit quietly and remember, but the crush of daily details makes me want to explode." I am disappointed that others rarely mention John's name or feel comfortable talking about him when thoughts of him are always present for me. The girls and I continue with our jobs.

In the depression that accompanies this terrible loss, I begin to face the fact that I have less control of my life than I once believed. My power to determine its path is very limited, and many of my questions are without answers. One of the few choices I do have is how I will respond to this crisis. In my loneliness, I am aware of a Presence that I know is God and begin to pray again: for my girls and for myself. I also recognize that God's angels are the people who surround and support us.

To neglect to pray for those in need is like leaving the scene of an accident.
—LaVerna Klippenstein

What makes this first summer bearable are those hands which reach out to us with love and caring. One Sunday afternoon two of John's high school classmates come to reminisce about their friendship with him. It is good to know that others are missing him. Friends invite us to their homes or to a restaurant, and eating together feels like communion. Married friends invite me to plays and concerts, giving the natural gift of friendship with both sexes that I have known for the past twenty-five years. Friends from a distance and my sisters phone regularly. Encouraging notes arrive weekly from a friend in the church and continue the entire first year. On John's birthday, a day when he is especially

Nothing ever happens to us alone. It happens to God too.
—Madeleine L'Engle

missed, flowers are delivered from friends in Ohio. One weekend a friend of Heidi and Kristin takes them to the Atlantic shore, a good break from the sadness at home. Others come to repair a broken brick on the porch steps, to help paint the fence, or to plant roses and impatiens in our flower gardens.

How to Be Helpful the First Year

1. Share meals with your friend, either in your home or in a restaurant. Sundays are especially lonely. Continue to invite your single friend to participate in activities with couples. He or she misses interaction with both sexes and will feel hurt if you sever your friendship because your friend no longer has a spouse.

2. The phrase, "Let me know if I can do anything," is not helpful. Make concrete offers such as, "There will be a plate for you on our table every Thursday evening," or "I'm free on Saturday and can help you with your storm windows." Try to think what your spouse would need if something happened to you.

3. Sympathy cards and notes are never late and may be more appreciated after the funeral flowers have faded and the mourners have returned home.

4. Assure the family who is preoccupied with their loss that you are missing their loved one too.

5. Pray for the family and tell them you are remembering them.

6. If the family includes children, offer to relieve the single parent or treat the children to special activities.

7. Call your friend periodically to check on his or her progress through grief and to assess needs, including financial ones.

8. Suggest grief counseling or support groups if the depressive phase of the grief process is prolonged. Allow your friend to grieve at his or her own pace.

9. Give a hug. Your friend is missing human touch.

10. Suggest or buy books on grief recovery for your friend.

11. Listen carefully to what your friend says he or she needs.

12. If you are knowledgeable in budgeting, investments, cooking, gardening/landscaping, or car maintenance, offer to advise or teach the spouse, forced to learn a new skill.

13. Mark the date of death on your calendar, then send a card or flowers on the first anniversary.

14. Be a sounding board for your friend, nearly overwhelmed by emotions and new decisions to be faced alone.

From Psalm 21

I raise my voice in praise, O God,

Because no one can separate me from You.

Though circumstances threaten me

And my own obsessions entangle me,

You will never let me go.

Your great power is sufficient to set me free

From these things that hurt my soul.

If I put my trust in You,

You will not allow them to destroy me,

I find so many reasons for praising You, O God.

—Leslie Brandt

The Second Year

Naively, I once believed that one passes through each grief stage, is healed, then goes on with life. I am not prepared for the emotional fluctuations of the second year. John is not coming back; his chair is permanently empty. I long for the normalcy we once knew and quietly shed a few tears nearly every Sunday in church, as I sit amidst intact families. Themes of grief, loss, and comfort in the music touch me deeply. I am tempted to stay at home on Sunday mornings but know instinctively that my wounded spirit needs nurture and community.

A nursing colleague is very helpful to me. She has been deeply hurt by a divorce and custody battle. Recognizing that I am trying to sort out how to support my family and where to live, she advises, "Define your boundaries, what you have the energy to do and what you can't manage." It soon becomes apparent that I cannot survive financially with two part-time jobs and no benefits. Driving thirty miles to work in a variety of weather conditions is stressful, and maintaining a nine-room farmhouse with a large yard and flower gardens is too difficult for one person. The first summer we clean out the attic and basement, discarding or giving away items we no longer need. John's sports equipment finds a home with relatives and friends. Heidi and Kristin sort through their childhood books and toys, and we pack them in boxes. John's clothing is donated to a resale shop whose proceeds are used to assist with development in poor countries. His theology books are delivered to Books Abroad, an endeavor of our church to expand the libraries of overseas schools.

Entrust the past to God's mercy, the present to His love, the future to His providence.

—St. Augustine

My journal records the internal struggle, even as we work to sort and pack some of our possessions:

> The fog of
> Grief
> Clings like an
> Unshakable
> Blanket.
>
> The gravestone
> Is there now

Marking
Your presence
In this
World,
But the cold, gray
Marble
Can never
Mark your
Life
Within us.

The regrets of our life together—trips not taken, sharp words, my reluctance to adapt to our living situation—mingle with the happy memories. All relationships are flawed, no matter how authentic or loving. My journal records my intent to be more affirming in the relationships which remain, and eventually I have the courage to identify with my daughters and to feel some of their pain. They have lost John's wisdom and understanding; they will miss the proud sparkle in his blue eyes at graduation. Who will host their weddings? Their children will never know him.

Some ability to concentrate returns. Reluctantly I leave Heidi, standing on the curb beside her dormitory in a run-down west Philadelphia neighborhood to begin her pharmacy studies. We have just carried most of her belongings to the third floor.

Kristin enters her senior year of high school.

The second summer after John's death, Kristin chooses to work at Ocean City, Maryland. A friend who is to accompany her pulls out at the last minute, but Kristin insists that walking on the beach and the lap of the waves "will help me get my head together." She is still grieving the loss of the two most important men in her life. With apprehension I watch her drive away alone. Heidi finds a job in Philadelphia. I identify a replacement and she is hired to manage the elderly housing complex, but I continue to work part-time in the evening on the hospice unit. It takes all summer to sort and pack our belongings. Friends offer to help, so I let them pack china or wash windows.

Growth always involves some pain, some stretching and changing.

—Delores Friesen

In June I visit my mother in Indiana, find a nursing position in long-term care, and purchase a condominium—all in two days! This is my first experience with a mortgage or buying property. Kristin will attend college in this Indiana town. Other relatives and friends live in the area, so living here seems to be a logical choice. The Pennsylvania farmhouse to which John and I gave so much time and energy is rented to a friend's daughter. As we drive away in our loaded car, it feels like another death. We stop at the local veterinarian with our beloved cat that is dying of old age to have her put to sleep. Kristin carries her into the vet with tears streaming down her cheeks. We cry half the way to Pittsburgh.

My cousin's husband engineers our move, renting the U-Haul and loading it with the help of volunteers. A friend prepares lunch for us and the moving crew. Then the truck is driven to Indiana and its contents unloaded with other volunteers into our brand-new condominium. The beds are set up, ready for use when we arrive, and there are a few groceries on the shelves. Without such a team effort of friends and family, this move would have been difficult indeed.

Even though leaving our familiar roots a year and a half after John's death may seem hasty, the decision has been a good one. It has greatly simplified my life, though there will be many adjustments and even a job change until I truly feel "settled."

Do not be anxious about anything, but in everything by prayer and petition, with thanksgiving, present your requests to God. And the peace of God which transcends all understanding, will guard your hearts and your minds in Christ Jesus.
—Philippians 4:6-7

How to Be Helpful During the Second Year

1. Do not urge your friend to "get on with life." The enormity of the loss is just beginning to become real. Let grieving persons cope and transition at their own pace. Grieving is hard work. It takes energy and a long time for most people.

2. Continue to invite him or her to eat with you or to attend special events. It takes energy to initiate social occasions for grieving persons, and they may fear you will have other plans.

3. If you have the skills, offer to do home repairs. Let your friend reimburse you, if the suggestion is made.

4. If a move becomes necessary, offer to prepare a meal for the movers or load the moving van. Offer to help pack boxes or to clean either house.

5. Continue to pray for the bereaved and their family.

6. Children need more role models than one parent can provide. Give them the experience of activities with an intact family.

7. Notes of love and encouragement are always appreciated.

8. Hugs are still important.

9. Be prepared for anger or depression in your friend. These are normal stages of the grief process. They may move back and forth between the stages of grief, so that you never know what to expect. Continue to listen so that your friend has a place to express feelings and to work out solutions. Do not take outbursts or withdrawal personally, and continue to communicate that you care.

When we walk to the edge of all the light
we have and take that step into the darkness of the
unknown, we must believe that one of two things
will happen – there will be something solid for us to
stand on, or we will be taught how to fly.

—Patrick Overton

Adjustment

Most of the grief literature says that the final stage of grief is acceptance. I believe a better word is adjustment. It makes no sense that John died at fifty-two, in the prime of his life. I have not found it possible to accept his death, but it *has* happened and I must adjust to it. I will always regret that our common dreams were lost; my task now is to form new dreams.

Most surprising has been how much changes after the death of a spouse or any loved one—nothing is the same. An uncle who lost a thirty-six-year-old son in an auto accident told me, "Life has lost some of its sparkle," and I must confess that it has been the same for me. It has been life-changing to feel how deeply sorrow can move into one's being.

Grief does not only invite change; it demands it. Losing John is not an experience I would have chosen, but with careful grief work, his loss has deepened my life. It is easier to be more aware and compassionate toward those who have suffered a variety of losses. In myself are strength and abilities of which I was unaware, and I have used these to build a satisfying life. After about five years, I discovered that I was looking forward, instead of looking over my shoulder, and grief was no longer the dominant theme of my life. I have also found that singleness offers the rewards of independence and a more flexible schedule. And now there is the opportunity to read in bed at night.

> *It is not what happens to us that matters as much as what happens in us.*
> —Gerald Sittser

Though my relationship with John greatly enriched my life, I realize he was not perfect. I had difficulty with the way he handled anger and the lack of mutuality in our decision making. He was also an impatient waiter. Childcare could have been more of a shared responsibility, a fact that he also recognized. He once said, "If I could do it over again, I would have been on fewer committees when the girls were young."

> *God, go before me to show me the way, above me to watch over me, beside me to be my constant companion, and within me to give me peace.*
> —Lloyd Ogilive

In my personal grief work, the God I have met does not protect us from pain but provides the faith and the inner resources to heal our wounds. God knows grief intimately and offers what we need to recover our equilibrium in ways that we can understand. Being a part of a Christian community that practices communal support is a rare gift in a fast-moving age.

When I was raging at God against John's loss, the loving care of friends and family was all that I could accept and the only way to be comforted. Later, I realized who motivated and sent them. David's laments in the Psalms took on new significance, especially as interpreted by Leslie Brandt in *Psalms Now*. Gradually uncertainty and doubt gave way to a deep sense of God's presence, and I feel gratitude for the generosity of God's love in the midst of my anger and alienation.

Hope is the thing with feathers
That perches in the soul
And sings the tune without
the words
And never stops at all.
—Emily Dickinson

I believe we need to bear in mind that death is only one source of grief. It is my observation that divorce, chronic pain, job losses, the birth of an unhealthy child, or debilitating illness or accidents can cause distress, far greater than the death of a loved one. A friend who lost his first wife to death and his second to separation found separation to be the most painful: "Death is an amputation; separation is like having gangrene." (I would note that people who experience these losses receive far less community support than the bereaved and would welcome the kinds of assistance suggested here.)

Heidi and Kristin both have completed college and graduate school and have married. We welcomed Jonathan, then Fran into our family with joy. John was especially missed at their graduations and weddings, and a single red rose in his memory commanded a prominent place near the altar at both weddings.

A Christian community is therefore a healing community, not because wounds are cured and pains alleviated but because wounds and pains become openings or occasions for a new vision ... and sharing weakness becomes a reminder of the coming strength.
—Henri Nouwen

My daughters and I phone or e-mail weekly, and the family gathers together as often as our budgets and schedules allow.

With John's death anniversary comes remembrance and sadness. But there is also thanksgiving for the years we had together rather than longing for what can never be. Slowly, in our own ways and in our own time, we are finding peace and healing, thanks to the kindness of those who shared our pain as they walked beside us.

How to Be Continually Supportive

1. Mention the deceased by name and listen as the bereaved talks about the loved one.

2. Point out the progress you have noted in your friend's grief process.

3. Ask questions such as: (a) What was John like? (if you did not know the deceased) or (b) What have you learned from your grief experience?

5. Provide opportunities for your friends to tell their stories and share their journey in group settings or to others who have been bereaved, if that is comfortable for them.

6. Keep in mind that there will still be remembrance as the death date approaches, no matter how many years have passed. Acknowledge their sadness with a card, note, or phone call.

7. Listen supportively as your friend explores new experiences and relationships.

Two are better than one . . . if they fall, one will lift up the other; but woe to one who is alone and falls and does not have another to help.

—Ecclesiastes 4:9-10

Epilogue

Seven years after John's death, I went to Belfast, Northern Ireland, to work with those who have lost loved ones in the thirty years of conflict there, called "The Troubles." Even though intentional murders are quite different from accidental deaths and evoke stronger emotions, the pain of grief and loss and the adjustments to life without the loved one are similar. Rather than being overwhelmed by the layers of grief in this troubled land, I was inspired by the stories of survival of the victims, by the humor of the people there, and by the triumph of the human spirit. The blessings of cross-community friendships, which recognize that Catholic and Protestant tears have a commonality, have been a gift to me and have helped me to believe that there is always hope for reconciliation when we can become vulnerable enough to share our personal pain. It is in the crucible of our powerlessness that God's work can take place.

Resources

Books

Inspirational

Albom, Mitch. *Tuesdays with Morrie*. New York: Doubleday, 1997.
    A student's memoirs of his mentor and favorite teacher's last days.
Bell, John L. *The Last Journey: Reflections for the Time of Grieving*. Chicago:
    GIA Publications, 1996.
        A member of the Iona Community in Scotland, Bell has gathered
        Scripture, prayers, and poetry into a gift book. Includes an audio recording
        of Bell's poetry, set to music and sung by the Cathedral Singers of Chicago.
Brandt, Leslie. *Psalms Now*. St. Louis: Concordia, 1973.
    The Psalms in contemporary, paraphrased language.
Brisco, Jill. *Out of the Storm and Into God's Arms*. Colorado Springs:
    Waterbrook Press, 2000.
        Using the biblical Job's questions and experiences, this popular writer
        and speaker discusses living in hope without demanding answers to the why
        questions. Includes interactive discussion questions and prayer suggestions
        for individual and small group use.

Clem, Dale. *A Moment with God for Those Who Grieve*. Nashville: Dimension
    For Living, 1999.
        A small book of scripture and short prayers for those who hurt.
Elliot, Elisabeth. *The Path of Loneliness: Finding Your Way Through the
    Wilderness to God*. Ann Arbor, Mich.: Servant Publications, 2001.
        This well-known Christian author and widow challenges those facing
    the loneliness of grief to tend the inner life.
Mehl, Ron. *What God Whispers in the Night*. Sisters, Ore.: Multnomah, 2000.
        A pastor reminds us that God is with us, is at work, and is awake
    during our darkest hours.
Moffat, Mary Jane, ed. *In the Midst of Winter: Selections from the Literature of
    Mourning*. New York: Vintage Books, 1992.
        A collection of great writings, including biblical, throughout the ages.
Powers, Margaret Fishback. *Footprints: Images and Reflections of God's Presence
    in Our Lives*. Grand Rapids, Mich.: Zondervan, 1999.
        Based on the well-known poem, "Footprints," this beautifully
    illustrated gift book interweaves scripture, song texts, and meditations to
    assure the reader that God is ever-present.

Death of a Child

D'Arcy, Paula. *Song for Sarah*. Colorado Springs: Waterbrook Press, 2001.
        Journal entries that begin before Sarah's birth and continue after the
    deaths of Sarah and her father in an auto accident. A poignant epilogue,
    written by Sarah's sister, adds insight into how children are affected by tragedy.
Froehlich, Mary Ann. *An Early Journey Home: Helping Families Work Through
    the Loss of a Child*. Grand Rapids, Mich.: Discovery House, 2000.
        A music therapist who works with terminally ill children shares her
    journal entries and suggests ways to comfort grieving families.
Wolterstorff, Nicholas. *Lament for a Son*. Grand Rapids, Mich.: Eerdmans, 1987.
        Personal and emotive reflections of a father who lost his son in a
    mountain climbing accident.

Suicidal Death

Carlson, Trudy. *Suicide Survivors Handbook: A Guide to the Bereaved and Those Who Wish to Help Them.* Duluth, Minn.: Benline Press, 1995.
>A mother's loss of her 14-year-old son to suicide inspires this comprehensive guide.

Fine, Carla. *No Time to Say Good-bye: Surviving the Suicide of a Loved One.* New York: Doubleday, 1997.
>The author's young, physician husband killed himself. She describes the emotional turmoil and stigma in a frank manner, using her own experiences and those of other survivors as well as guidance from mental health professionals.

Comfort for the Bereaved

Bauman, Harold. *Grief's Slow Work.* Scottdale: Herald Press, 1960.
>The author encourages the bereaved to feel the hurt and to express it, not rushing the process—based on the stages of grief.

Brothers, Dr. Joyce. *Widowed.* New York: Simon & Schuster, 1990.
>A popular psychologist and author shares her own feelings of being lost after the death of her husband and tells how she came to embrace life again.

Coleman, William and Patricia. *"Dear God It Hurts!" (Comfort for Those Who Grieve).* Ann Arbor, Mich.: Servant Publications, 2000.
>Brief stories and pithy quotations are useful for the newly bereaved with short attention spans.

Felber, Marta. *Finding Your Way After Your Spouse Dies.* Notre Dame, Ind.: Ave Maria Press, 2000.
>A "how to" book on managing grief and changes after the death of a spouse.

Firzgerald, Helen, *The Mourning Handbook.* New York: Simon & Schuster, 1994.
>A therapist and certified death educator who has grieved the death of a husband has compiled a comprehensive and practical resource for the bereaved.

Froehlich, Mary Ann and Peggy Sue Wells. *What to Do When You Don't Know What to Say.* Minneapolis, Minn.: Bethany House, 2000.
> Short vignettes of ways people become Jesus' hands to others in times of loss—instructive about which acts are truly helpful.

Gibbs, Terri, ed. *Deeper Than Tears: Promises of Comfort and Hope.* Nashville: J. Countryman, 1999.
> A tapestry of Scripture, short quotations of famous people, and stunning nature photography.

Ginsburg, Genevieve Davis. *Widow to Widow: Thoughtful, Practical Ideas for Rebuilding Your Life.* Tucson, Ariz.: Fisher Books, 1997.
> A helpful guide for the early weeks after the death of a spouse and beyond.

Kubler-Ross, Elizabeth. *On Death and Dying.* New York: Macmillan, 1993.
> A classic that details the various stages of grief.

Kushner, Rabbi Harold. *When Bad Things Happen to Good People.* New York: Schocken Books, 1981.
> A book for those who are angry at God and are asking the why questions.

Lambin, Helen Reichert. *The Death of a Husband: Reflections for a Grieving Wife.* Chicago: ACTA Publications, 1998.
> Poetry revealing the real feelings which accompany various aspects of grief.

L'Engle, Madeleine. *Two Part Invention: The Story of a Marriage.* New York: Farrar, Straus & Giroux, 1988.
> Beloved author, Madeleine L'Engle was married to actor, Hugh Franklin. This is the story of that marriage, Hugh's death from cancer, the pain of his death, and the solace L'Engle found.

Lewis, C. S. *A Grief Observed.* Greenwich, Conn.: Seabury Press, 1963.
> The author was married to Joy Davidman for a brief time. He candidly shares his grief, never losing sight of God, and comes to profound understandings about the meaning of suffering.

Manning, Doug. *Don't Take My Grief Away from Me: How to Walk Through Grief and Learn to Live Again.* Oklahoma City: Insight Press, 1999.
> Practical guide for dealing with the emotional and decision-making aspects of grief.

Nouwen, Henri. *Can You Drink This Cup?* Notre Dame, Ind.: Ave Maria Press, 1966.
> A wise spiritual father explains how the cup of sorrow and the cup of joy are related, helping to put grief into perspective.

Sittser, Gerald. *A Grace Disguised: How the Soul Grows Through Loss.*
Grand Rapids, Mich.: Zondervan, 1996.
    An inspirational book about one man's grief work after the deaths
of his wife, daughter, and mother from an auto accident in which he was
the driver.
Weems, Ann. *Psalms of Lament.* Louisville, Ky.: Westminister/John Knox Press,
1995.
    These psalms emerge from the depths of the author's grief about the
death of her son. A book "for those who are living with scalding tears
running down their cheeks."
Westberg, Granger. *Good Grief.* Philadelphia: Fortress Press, 1971.
    A small booklet by a pioneer in holistic health care which describes the
patterns of grief and what can be learned from grief itself.
Zonnebelt-Smeege, Susan and Robert DeVries. *Getting to the Other Side of Grief:
Overcoming the Loss of a Spouse.* Grand Rapids, Mich.: Baker Books, 1998.
    A book to be read several months after the death of a spouse. Practical
suggestions from a nurse/psychologist and a pastor for new relationships
after grief work has been done.

MAGAZINES

Bereavement Magazine, Bereavement Publishing, Inc., 5125 North
Union Boulevard, Colorado Springs, CO 80918.

WEB SITES

Bereaved Parents of the USA—
    http://www.bereavedparentsusa.org./links/links.htm/
    Home page of the organization, Bereaved Parents of the USA. Provides
a link to related bereavement web sites.
Bereavement Publishing—http://www.bereavementmag.com/
    Includes an online magazine, e-sympathy cards, booklets that can be
read online, gifts, and more.
Family Bereavement—http://www.parentsplace.com/family/bereavement
    Resources for losses in families ranging from miscarriage to the death of
a pet.

Grief and Bereavement World Wide Web Links—
    http://www.grief.org.au/internet/.htm
        A comprehensive guide to web resources around the world for the bereaved and those who care for them.
Grief Works—http://www.griefworks.com/
        Website which offers an extensive grief book list as well as a list of books about coping with cancer.
The Grief and Bereavement Channel—
    http://www.brooknoel.com/griefmain.htm/
        Includes the book *I Wasn't Ready to Say Goodbye: Surviving, Coping and Healing After the Death of a Loved One* and a monthly newsletter.
What to Do When the Police Leave—
    http://www.willsworld.com/online.htm
        A guide for the first days of traumatic loss.
Wings—http://www.wingsgrief.org
        An information site for caregivers and the bereaved. Includes a newsletter and list of bereavement organizations.

About the Author

Sara Wengerd is a registered nurse who has worked in obstetrics, geriatrics, hospice, and psychiatry. In 2001 she finished an assignment with Mennonite Central Committee, working with those bereaved by the civil war in Northern Ireland. Her book of interviews from those three years in Belfast, *Crossings: Long-term Perspectives of the Troubles*, was recently published.

Wengerd lives in Goshen, Indiana, and is the mother of two adult daughters. She is a member of the Goshen College Mennonite Church.